Novel Unit for

A Long Walk To Water

By

Linda Sue Park

Resources Created & Compiled by

Sarah Pennington

Table of Contents

Table of Contents Continued

Common Core Anchor Standards for Language Arts (Grades 6-12) In This Novel Unit

Reading:

1. Read closely to determine what the text says explicitly and to make logical inferences from it; cite specific textual evidence when writing or speaking to support conclusions drawn from the text.

2. Determine central ideas or themes of a text and analyze their development; summarize the key supporting details and ideas.

3. Analyze how and why individuals, events, and ideas develop and interact over the course of a text.

5. Analyze the structure of texts, including how specific sentences, paragraphs, and larger portions of the text (e.g., a section, chapter, scene, or stanza) relate to each other and the whole.

10. Read and comprehend complex literary and informational texts independently and proficiently.

Writing:

1. Write arguments to support claims in an analysis of substantive topics or texts, using valid reasoning and relevant and sufficient evidence.

2. Write informative/explanatory texts to examine and convey complex ideas and information clearly and accurately through the effective selection, organization, and analysis of content.

3. Write narratives to develop real or imagined experiences or events using effective technique, well-chosen details, and well-structured event sequences.

4. Produce clear and coherent writing in which the development, organization, and style are appropriate to task, purpose, and audience.

7. Conduct short as well as more sustained research projects based on focused questions, demonstrating understanding of the subject under investigation.

8. Gather relevant information from multiple print and digital sources, assess the credibility and accuracy of each source, and integrate the information while avoiding plagiarism.

9. Draw evidence from literary or informational texts to support analysis, reflection, and research.

10. Write routinely over extended time frames (time for research, reflection, and revision) and shorter time frames (a single sitting or a day or two) for a range of tasks, purposes, and audiences.

Speaking & Listening:

1. Prepare for and participate effectively in a range of conversations and collaborations with diverse partners, building on others' ideas and expressing their own clearly and persuasively.

4. Present information, findings, and supporting evidence such that listeners can follow the line of reasoning and the organization, development, and style are appropriate to task, purpose, and audience.

5. Make strategic use of digital media and visual displays of data to express information and enhance understanding of presentations.

Summary of the Story:

A Long Walk To Water is actually composed of two narratives that eventually weave together.

The first part of each chapter tells the story of Nya, a young girl growing up in southern Sudan in 2008. Nya must walk each day to a small pond to get water for her family during the rainy season. During the dry season, her family moves closer to a lake where Nya must dig deep into the clay lake bed to get water for her family. During the course of the story, Nya's sister gets sick from the water they drink, which is dirty and muddy.

Life in Nya's village changes when a pair of men in a jeep come to visit. They have come to drill a well so that the village and the people near-by can have clean water to drink. With the well built, Nya will no longer have to walk the long distance to the pond to get water and will now be able to go to school.

The second part of each chapter tells the story of Salva Dut, one of the Lost Boys of Sudan. As Salva is sitting in school one day in 1985, gunfire erupts nearby. He and his classmates escape into the bush. Salva spends the next ten years or so traveling and settling in various refugee camps, running from the violence of his nation's civil war. In the process, he sees his uncle killed, is chased by soldiers into a crocodile-infested river, and becomes the leader of over 1000 young boys looking for a safe refuge.

Eventually Salva finds a home in Rochester, New York. But he finds a purpose after he returns to Sudan to visit his father in a clinic where he is recovering from surgery. After so many years of drinking dirty water, Salva's father had become dangerously ill. Salva makes it his mission to bring clean water to the people of southern Sudan.

The two stories connect beautifully at the end when Nya goes to thank the man who leads the drilling crew. Even though he is from an enemy tribe, he has come to her village to help them. The man introduces himself to her: his name is Salva.

Before Reading Activity Suggestions:

- Have students read about the author, Linda Sue Park. A good starting point is her web site, http://www.lindasuepark.com/

- Learn about Sudan, the tribes of Sudan, and the Second Sudanese Civil War. Basic information, links, and activities are included in this novel guide.

- Do a cover study. Have students study the front cover and make a list of the various images and details they notice. What does this tell them about the book? What predictions can they make about the book based on the cover?

- Do a word sort. Choose some words from the book and ask students to sort them into categories. You can assign the categories or allow students to create their own. Once the words are sorted, ask the students to predict what the story will be about based on the words they just sorted.
  Possible words for word sort:

Water	Desert	War	Barn	Walk
Lost	Refugee	Ethiopia	Exhaustion	Crocodile
Gun	Mosquito	Mango	Bees	Thorn

During Reading Activity Suggestions:

- Students can complete a conflict map as they read. For each chapter, have the student list at least one conflict and tell if that conflict is an example of an internal or external conflict. (Charts for this activity are included on pages 23-26 of this guide. Two charts are included to meet the needs of various student levels.)

- Focus on theme. This can be done as a whole class activity, or you can divide the class into small groups and give each group a theme to focus on. (When I do this, I also choose a theme and do the activity for each chapter to model.) For each chapter, have students note what events and ideas in that chapter apply to the chosen theme. This can be recorded on a chart, added to a bulletin board using sticky notes, etc. At the end of the novel, students can use the notes to answer the following question: What was the author's message about your theme? (For example, if the chosen theme was "Family," what is Park saying about family and what information from the text supports this message?)
  Possible themes:
  Family   Survival   War   Grief   Kindness
  Coming of Age   Persistence

- Complete a plot map—after each chapter, ask students to add the chapter to a plot map to indicate if that chapter was part of the exposition, rising action, etc. Since this novel has two stories within it, students can create a separate plot map for each story line.

- Chart Salva's course throughout the book. Find a map of Sudan and the surrounding countries for this purpose.

Sudan Quick Facts:

- The Republic of Sudan is the largest country in Africa (1,861,484 square miles)

- Sixteenth largest country in the world by area

- Bordered on the north by Egypt, on the northwest by Libya, on the southeast by Uganda and Kenya, on the southwest by the Democratic Republic of the Congo and the Central African Republic, on the east by Ethiopia and Eritrea, and on the west by Chad.

- Capital is Khartoum

- After achieving independence from Egypt and Great Britain in 1956, Sudan went through a 17 year period of civil war between the Northern people of Sudan (mainly Arabic & Islamist) and the Southern people of Sudan (Christian and tribal religions). This war ended in 1972.

- The Second Sudanese Civil War (the setting of one of the novel's story lines) began in 1983.

- Sudan is divided into 15 states.

- The northern part of Sudan is dryer, with a three-month rainy season, while the southern part has a six-month rainy season. Because of this, southern Sudan has swamps and rainforests, whereas northern Sudan is mostly desert.

- The official languages of Sudan are Arabic and English.

As of July 2011, South Sudan is an independent nation, and is about the size of Texas. There are very few sources updated to reflect this change. The geographic information above refers to Sudan before South Sudan split from the northern part of the country.

Information from:

"Background Note: Sudan." *U.S. Department of State*. U.S. Department of State, January 10, 2012. Web. 25 Jul 2012. <http://www.state.gov/r/pa/ei/bgn/5424.htm>.

"Sudan." *The World Factbook*. Central Intelligence Agency, July 17, 2012. Web. 25 Jul 2012. <https://www.cia.gov/library/publications/the-world-factbook/geos/su.html>.

"Transforming Lives in South Sudan." *Water for South Sudan*. Water for South Sudan, Inc., 2011. Web. 25 Jul 2012. <http://www.waterforsouthsudan.org/mission/>.

Chapter 1

Comprehension Questions:

1. This novel has two different story lines within it. Who is the main character of the first story line (Sudan, 2008)?

2. How old is this character?

3. Who is the main character of the second story line (Sudan, 1985)?

4. Where is this character (specifically) when his story begins?

5. What is this character's tribe called?

6. How old is this character?

7. In what way does this character realize he is lucky?

8. Describe this character's family.

9. What does this character look forward to getting when he gets home?

10. What happens that interrupts this character's normal day?

11. Where does this character and the others with him go?

12. What is happening where this character lives?

Extension/Discussion Questions:

1. Based on the first chapter and the title of the novel, where is Nya going? Use evidence from the story to support your answer.

> **Who are the Dinka?**
>
> The Dinka are one of many tribes that live in Sudan. The tribe's main employment is through cattle herding and the growing of crops, including millet.
>
> The Dinka religion is monotheistic (believes in one god) and their god is called Nhialic.
>
> Upon reaching adulthood, Dinka males are marked with large gashes that form a pattern of scars. Women are also decorated through this process of scarification.
>
> *For more information:*
> http://www.everyculture.com/wc/Rwanda-to-Syria/Dinka.html
>
> http://www.wydasudan.org/dinka-tribe/

Chapter 2

Comprehension Questions:

1. What happens to Nya in this chapter?

2. How do the people walking along with Salva choose to divide themselves up?

3. What is the name of Salva's village?

4. What do the soldiers do with the people?

5. What does Salva try to do in the rebel camp?

6. What happens to the men the next morning?

7. Where do the women and children sleep after leaving the rebel camp?

8. What has happened to Salva when he awakes after an itchy night in the hay?

"A soldier approached Salva and raised his gun."

Extension/Discussion Questions:

1. Why do you think the other people left Salva behind? How do you feel about this choice?

Language Activity: Why is it called a "Civil" War?

The word "civil" has many definitions. Look at the following definitions for the word and choose which meaning is used in the term "Civil War." Then discuss how the idea of a "Civil War" could be different if another definition of "civil" were intended for use in the term.

Civil (adj)
1. courteous, polite

2. of the state or nation

3. consisting of citizens

4. showing benevolence

What other terms could be used in place of "Civil War" that would still have the same meaning, showing that the war was taking place between groups within a nation?

Chapter 3

Comprehension Questions:

1. Describe the pond where Nya gets water.

2. Does the water Nya gets sound good to drink? Explain.

3. How does Nya carry the water home?

4. Why does Salva think the others left him behind?

5. What does Salva see when he leaves the barn?

6. How does he know the woman is part of his tribe?

7. What does the woman give Salva when he first approaches her?

8. How long does Salva stay with the woman?

9. Why do Salva and the woman have to separate?

10. What does Salva hear as he sits in the barn pondering the woman's words?

Extension/Discussion Questions:

1. Salva is relived that the woman is a member of the same tribe as he. However, he is still unsure if she will be friendly toward him when he approaches. Why might the woman be unfriendly toward a child from her own tribe?

Organizing the Text: Chronological Order

A Long Walk To Water is written in chronological (time) order.

- What does the author do to help the reader see this?

- Why do you think the author chooses to write the novel in this way?

Chapter 4

Comprehension Questions:

1. What does Nya's mother do with the water?

2. What does Nya have to eat when she returns home?

3. What does her mother tell Nya to do on her next trip to the pond?

4. What do the strangers say when the old woman asks them to take Salva with them?

5. Why does one man agree to bring Salva with them?

6. What does the old woman give Salva before he leaves with the others?

7. Who else joins the group after about a week of walking?

8. Who is the young man that Salva walks next to on the day the group eats well?

9. Who finds food for the group and what food does this person find?

Extension/Discussion Questions:

1. Why does Nya not want to take her little sister to the pond with her? How does this relate to Salva's situation?

Narrative Writing: Siblings

Nya has to take her little sister along with her when she returns to the pond, although she doesn't want to. Have you ever had to take a younger sibling or other relative with you when you didn't want to?

Write a story in which you have to take a younger sibling with you somewhere. How might the sibling's presence change your plans? Will you act differently if you have a younger child with you? (If you do not have younger siblings, use your imagination!)

Chapter 5

Comprehension Questions:

1. How far from Nya's village is the big lake?

2. Why doesn't Nya's family live near the big lake all the time?

3. How does Nya fetch water at the lake?

4. What happened when the group tried to get the honey from the beehive?

5. Why can one man not enjoy the honey?

6. How does Salva meet Marial?

7. Where is the group headed?

8. What do the Dinka call the Atuot and why?

Extension/Discussion Questions:

1. How do you think Salva's journey will be different now that he has made a friend?

Science Connection: Bees

The discovery of a bee hive is a cause for celebration for Salva and his companions. Research to discover the following:

◊ What species of bee is found in southern Sudan?

◊ Do bees see in color?

◊ Is honey straight from a bee hive safe to eat?

◊ How long has mankind used honey as a food?

◊ How long will honey stay fresh?

Chapter 6

Comprehension Questions:

1. What does Nya like about the camp at the lake?

2. What is Nya's mother afraid of when the family is at the lake camp?

3. Who calls Salva's name?

4. How long had this person been walking with the group before finding Salva?

5. What does this person have that makes him useful to the group?

6. What causes Salva to be up sick most of a night?

7. What does this person tell Salva after Salva and the group have slept just off the path following a ten hour all-night walk?

"Would they be lucky again?

Or was it now their turn to lose someone?"

Extension/Discussion Questions:

1. When Salva's uncle wakes him, Salva hears someone crying. What does this tell you about the situation?

Chapter 7

Comprehension Questions:

1. Why is Nya worried about her little sister, Akeer?

2. What choice is Nya's family faced with?

3. What does Salva think has happened to Marial?

4. What obstacle does the group need to cross to get to Ethiopia?

5. How does the group overcome this obstacle?

6. How does Salva help in this task?

Chapter 8

Comprehension Questions:

1. What choice does Nya's family make about Akeer's illness?

2. What is the family told to do to keep Akeer from getting sick again?

3. Why will this be difficult while the family is at the lake camp?

4. Where does Salva's group stop on their journey across the Nile?

5. What does Uncle share with Salva?

6. What does Salva remember his father bringing as a treat from the marketplace? What was special about the way this treat was transported?

7. What happens after all the fishermen go into their tents?

8. What warning are the travelers given about the next part of their journey?

Extension/Discussion Questions:

1. Salva is not sure if the fishermen share with Uncle because he has a gun or because he seems to be the leader of the group. Which do you feel is more likely? Explain.

Research Opportunity: Waterborne Diseases

According to the World Health Organization, waterborne diseases are the leading cause of death around the world.

Choose one of the suggested waterborne diseases and research the following:

- What are the symptoms?

- How wide-spread is this disease?

- How is it treated?

- How deadly is it?

- How can it be avoided?

Suggested diseases:

| Cholera | Typhoid | Guinea Worm | Dysentery |

Chapter 9

Comprehension Questions:

1. Who shows up in Nya's village and what do they talk about with the chief?

2. How long does Uncle say it will take to cross the desert?

3. What happens toward the end of their first day in the desert that makes it hard for Salva to continue?

4. How does Uncle keep Salva going?

5. What does the group find on the second day of their journey across the desert?

Extension/Discussion Questions:

1. When one of the women in the group gives water to one of the men they find in the desert, someone else tells her that she will die if she shares her water. Which do you feel is making a better decision: the woman who shares her water with another or the man who keeps his for himself to better insure his own survival? Explain.

> **Quick Research: How Long Can He Last?**
>
> Ask students to find answers for the following:
>
> - How long can a human being go without water?
>
> - What are the symptoms of dehydration?
>
> - How does dehydration affect the body?

Chapter 10

Comprehension Questions:

1. What do the men who visit the village say they will find between the two trees where the village usually gathers around a big fire?

2. What happens to the men that are given water by women in the group?

3. What does Salva ask Uncle on their third day in the desert? What is Uncle's response?

4. What else does Uncle tell Salva that upsets him?

5. What gives Salva a little hope that he might see his family again someday?

6. What does the group find by a small muddy pool of water?

7. What happens as the group is gathered around the muddy pool of water?

> *"Three shots rang out. Then the men ran away."*

Extension/Discussion Questions:

1. Salva wonders if he would have shared his water with those men if he were older and stronger, or would he have kept his water for himself? Based on what you know about Salva, which do you think he would have done. Explain using details from the story to support your answer.

2. For the first time on his journey, Salva sees a benefit to being the smallest of the group. How might things have been different for Salva if he had been bigger and older?

Chapter 11

Comprehension Questions:

1. What do the villagers begin working on after the two men in the jeep leave?

2. Where does the group bury Uncle?

3. What happened to the stork the group was cooking?

4. How does Salva feel now that Marial and Uncle are both gone?

5. How does the attitude of the group toward Salva change once Uncle is dead?

6. What does Salva see when he reaches the refugee camp?

7. Who does Salva think he sees on his second day in the camp?

Chapter 12

Comprehension Questions:

1. What is the red iron giraffe that is brought to the village?

2. What do the villagers do with the rocks that the women bring back to the village?

3. What does Salva realize as he is trying to catch up with the woman in the orange headscarf?

4. How long does Salva live at the refugee camp?

5. How old is Salva when the camp is closed?

6. Where do the soldiers chase the people of the camp?

7. What are the dangers of the place the people are being driven toward?

Background Information: Uprising in Ethiopia

The refugee camp is closed following an uprising against the government of Ethiopia. After living in safety at the camp for years, the refugees are driven out by a different civil war.

After the government of Ethiopia was overthrown in 1991, it took three years to write a new constitution.

For more information:

https://www.cia.gov/library/publications/the-world-factbook/geos/et.html

---

Chapter 13

Comprehension Questions:

1. What does Nya find funny about drilling for water?

2. What discourages the drilling crew?

3. Who keeps encouraging and pushing the workers to continue working?

4. What happens to the young man Salva watches jump into the river?

5. What forces Salva to finally jump into the water?

6. How does another boy accidentally save Salva's life?

7. Where does Salva decide to walk toward?

8. What happens as Salva is walking?

9. What does Salva decide the group needs to do to travel safely?

10. How many boys make it to Kenya? How long does it take?

Extension/Discussion Questions:

1. How do memories of his family help Salva get the group of boys safely to Kenya?

Chapter 14

Comprehension Questions:

1. What happens on the third afternoon of drilling in Nya's village?

2. What makes Nya frown as she watches the people celebrate?

3. How old is Salva in the beginning of this chapter?

4. What was Kakuma like?

5. How long did Salva stay at Kakuma?

6. Where does Salva go after he leaves Kakuma?

7. Who teaches Salva how to read and play volleyball?

8. What rumor begins spreading through the camps?

9. What sort of people will be given the opportunity Salva has heard about?

10. Where does the list say Salva is going?

Extension/Discussion Questions:

1. Salva learns to read and write English from an aid worker at the camp. How is the method Michael uses to teach Salva similar to the way you learned to read and write? How is it different?

Comprehension Questions:

1. Why does Dep say the water coming from the borehole is muddy?

2. What are the orphans live Salva from Sudan being called in America?

3. Where does Salva go from Ifo to prepare for his trip to America?

4. What one thing does Salva remember clearly from his preparations to go to America?

5. What does Salva have to drink on the airplane that reminds him of his family?

6. How many planes does Salva have to take to get to his new home?

7. Describe Salva's new family.

"Nya sighed and picked up the big plastic can. Yet another walk to the pond."

Extension/Discussion Questions:

1. Salva stops just before leaving the airport because he realizes he is leaving his old life behind him. After his long journey, why do you think this particular place and moment makes him have this realization?

Literature Connection: *Peter Pan*

The orphaned boys from Sudan have come to be called "Lost Boys." This is a reference to the book *Peter Pan* by J.M. Barrie.

In *Peter Pan*, the Lost Boys are a group of young orphans who join in Peter's adventures, fighting pirates and saving an Indian princess. Despite the fun and freedom they enjoy, the Lost Boys choose to leave Neverland at the end of the story and find families.

Why is this an appropriate name to give to boys like Salva?

Chapter 16

Comprehension Questions:

1. What do the men in the village start doing after the first spray of water?

2. What has Salva not seen in his first month in Rochester?

3. What does Salva focus on to block out the confusion of his new life?

4. How long had it taken Salva to get from Ifo to Rochester?

5. What does Salva decide to study in college?

6. Salva gets an e-mail from his cousin. What does this message tell him?

7. How long does it take to get Salva's trip back to Sudan organized?

Extension/Discussion Questions:

1. Salva has trouble learning English because of some of the words and sounds that change for no reason. Have you ever felt the same frustration that Salva feels? What are some examples from English that you find confusing?

2. As Salva is traveling through Sudan to see his father, he says that he remembered everything like it was yesterday, yet his memories of Sudan also feel distant. Explain what Salva means in your own words.

Chapter 17

Comprehension Questions:

1. What does Nya's father tell her is being built near the tree?

2. How long has it been since Salva and his father had seen each other?

3. What has happened to the rest of Salva's family?

4. What had made Salva's father sick?

5. What does Salva think about that helps him get over his stage fright the first time he speaks in front of an audience to raise funds for his project?

Extension/Discussion Questions:

1. Nya's father tells her that even the girls will be able to go to the new school. How does this show changes in Sudan since the time Salva was a child?

Chapter 18

Comprehension Questions:

1. What does the leader of the workers do before the villagers use the new well pump for the first time?

2. Who is working the well pump when Nya gets water? Why would this person be the one to work the pump this first day?

3. What other changes will be coming to the village because of the new well?

4. What does Dep tell Nya that surprises her?

5. What does Nya say to the leader of the work crew?

6. Who is the leader of the work crew?

> **Writing Activity: RAFT**
>
> RAFT stands for Role, Audience, Format, Topic
>
> Imagine you are Salva's father. You are writing a letter to your wife (Salva's mother) telling her that your son, Salva is alive and that you have seen him.
>
> See page 22 for a rubric that can be used for grading this and other RAFT projects. You can assign your own percentages to each category in the rubric to fit your goal(s) for the assignment.

A Message from Salva Dut

Comprehension Questions:

1. Who does Salva thank for helping him when he was in danger of starving?

2. Where did Salva go to college?

3. What is the name of Salva's project?

4. What two things does Salva say helped him overcome his difficulties?

Extension/Discission Questions:

1. Salva states that "Quitting leads to much less happiness in life than perseverance and hope." Can you think of other people (famous or in your own life) who would agree with this statement? Choose one of these people and discuss how Salva's statement applies to this person's life and accomplishments.

> For more information on Salva's organization:
>
> http://www.waterforsouthsudan.org/
>
> To see a video about Salva and his work:
>
> http://www.waterforsouthsudan.org/salvas-story/

Whole Novel Discussion Questions:

- The author tells the story of two people whose lives eventually intersect in this novel. Which of the two do you feel is the more important character? Explain.

- What do you feel is the biggest obstacle Salva had to overcome? Support your answer with details from the story.

- Salva's organization drills wells for people all over southern Sudan, even if they, like Nya's village, are from a different tribe than his own. What does this tell you about Salva's character? What lessons can be learned from Salva's choice to help others, even those who could be considered an "enemy?"

Post-Reading Activity Suggestions:

- Create a Venn Diagram or similar graphic organizer to compare and contrast Salva and Nya. This can be expanded into an essay or other assignment.

- Create a newspaper about the events in the novel. The newspaper can include a main article (summary of the novel), a human interest story (a character sketch of one of the characters and his/her role in the story), an advice column (what advice would one of the characters ask for and what would the student tell him/her?) and advertisements (what products might characters in the story need or want?).

- Create a book cover for the book. The front should have the book title and an image that relates to the novel, while the back should have a short "blurb" or summary of the novel that does not give away the ending.

- Create a talk show featuring characters from the story. Students can take the roles of the various characters and get "interviewed" by the talk show host about the events of the story and how they felt about the outcome.

- Write a letter to the author of the book. What would you like to tell her? Did you enjoy the book? Why or why not? What would you like to know that the book didn't quite tell you? Would you like to read more about the characters?

- Choose a scene from the story and turn it into a Reader's Theater script. Remember, a reader's theater script will feature one or more narrators telling the action of the story.

- Allow students to choose a quote or short section of the novel that they feel is important, funny, or makes them think. Put students in small groups to discuss the quotes chosen by each member, allowing each student to share his/her quote and tell why it was chosen, then giving other students an opportunity to share their thoughts about the quote.

- Create an ABC book about the novel. For each letter of the alphabet, come up with a person, place, event, etc. and explain how he/she/it is important in the novel. Draw a picture to go with each letter as well.

Rubric For Raft Activity

CATEGORY	4	3	2	1	0
Comprehension of Characters' Role in Story	Information in the writing shows that the student fully understands the character's role in the story. (Who is the character? What did he/she do in the story?) Student extends this knowledge to predict what that character may be doing in the future based on his/her previous role or to interpret the character's feelings.	Information in the writing shows that the student mostly understands the character's role in the story. (Who is the character? What did he/she do in the story?) Student extends this knowledge to predict what that character may be doing in the future based on his/her previous role or to interpret the character's feelings.	Information in the writing shows that the student basically understands the character's role in the story. (Who is the character? What did he/she do in the story?)	Information in the writing shows that the student knows who the characters are, but may not clearly understand their roles in the story.	Student has mixed up characters and/or their roles in the story.
Use of Story Details to Support Actions	Student discusses the character's feelings about the events of the story and how those events changed the character. Details about the event are used, instead of simply saying "What you did to me hurt me, etc."	Student mentions major events of the story and makes connections between these and the current behavior of the character.	Student mentions events in the story briefly, but does not clearly show how they affected the characters or caused them to change.	Student uses only very vague details about the events of the story or does show how the events of the story have affected the characters' behavior.	Student uses no details at all to support the characters' actions after the story.
Creative/ Imaginative Writing	Student's writing is creative/imaginative. Student has obviously put a great deal of thought into how the events of the story could drastically affect the characters and written them in an entertaining manner.	Student has put a good effort toward imagining the after-effects of the story events and how they affect the characters and has created a variety of possibilities that are presented in an entertaining fashion.	Student has spent some time attempting to ponder the effects of the story events and has included a couple of ways in which the characters may have been changed by their experiences and have written them in a way that interests the reader.	Student has put only minor thought into the writing, but has put in at least one consequence of the events not mentioned in the story itself. The manner in which it is written is bland.	Student has put no thought into the creation of the writing. The work was obviously done just to turn in a sheet of paper.
Grammar/ Spelling	No more than 2 errors in spelling, punctuation, and grammar.	Only 3-4 Spelling, grammar, and punctuation errors.	Only 5-6 errors in spelling, grammar, and punctuation.	Only 7-8 errors in spelling, grammar, and punctuation.	Nine or more errors in spelling, grammar, and punctuation.

Charting the Problems: Conflict Map

For each chapter, write down the parties involved in one conflict, then mark whether the conflict is internal or external. Chapter one has been completed for you.

Chapter	Conflict	Internal	External
1	Nya vs. the heat, time, and thorns Rebels vs. the government		X X
2	_____ vs. _____ _____ vs. _____		
3	_____ vs. _____ _____ vs. _____		
4	_____ vs. _____ _____ vs. _____		
5	_____ vs. _____ _____ vs. _____		
6	_____ vs. _____ _____ vs. _____		
7	_____ vs. _____ _____ vs. _____		
8	_____ vs. _____ _____ vs. _____		
9	_____ vs. _____ _____ vs. _____		

Chapter	Conflict	Internal	External
10	_____ vs. _____ _____ vs. _____		
11	_____ vs. _____ _____ vs. _____		
12	_____ vs. _____ _____ vs. _____		
13	_____ vs. _____ _____ vs. _____		
14	_____ vs. _____ _____ vs. _____		
15	_____ vs. _____ _____ vs. _____		
16	_____ vs. _____ _____ vs. _____		
17	_____ vs. _____ _____ vs. _____		
18	_____ vs. _____ _____ vs. _____		

Charting the Problems: Conflict Map

For each chapter, write down at least one conflict that occurred within the chapter, then mark whether the conflict was internal or external. Chapter one has been completed for you.

Chapter	Conflict	Internal	External
1	Nya has to walk a long way through the heat . People are rebelling against the Sudan government		X X
2			
3			
4			
5			
6			
7			
8			
9			

Chapter	Conflict	Internal	External
10			
11			
12			
13			
14			
15			
16			
17			
18		Internal	External

Answer Key for *A Long Walk to Water* Comprehension & Extension/Discussion Questions

Chapter 1 Comprehension Question Answers:

1. Nya is the main character of the first story line (2008).

2. Nya is eleven.

3. Salva is the main character of the second story line (1985).

4. Salva is at school when the story begins.

5. Salva is part of the Dinka tribe.

6. Salva is eleven.

7. Salva realizes that he is lucky to be able to attend school.

8. Salva's family is well-off compared to most around him. His father owns lots of cattle and is the judge in their village. He apparently has more than one wife, because it talks about "the sons of his father's other wives." Salva has three brothers and two sisters. His two older brothers are named Ariik and Ring, and his younger brother is Kuol. His sisters are named Akit and Agnath. His sisters stay home with their mother to learn how to keep house instead of going to school like Salva. The boys' job, when they are not in school or are not old enough to go to school yet, is to watch over the cattle.

9. Salva looks forward to getting a bowl of milk when he gets home because he is hungry.

10. Salva's day is interrupted when gunfire starts outside.

11. Salva and his classmates run into the bush, away from their village.

12. There is a civil war happening where Salva lives, with the people in the southern part of the country (where Salva lives) fighting against the government in the north, which wants all the people in the county to practice the same religion.

Chapter 1 Extension/Discussion Question Answers:

Based on the first chapter and the title of the novel, Nya is walking a long way to get water. The title of the book implies this, and Nya is carrying an empty plastic container, which she can use to carry the water back.

Chapter 2 Comprehension Question Answers:

1. She steps on a large thorn which gets stuck in her heel.

2. The people who are walking decide to divide up by village.

3. Salva's village is called Loun-Ariik.

4. The soldiers take the people to their camp, then separate the men from the women, children, and old people.

5. Salva tries to go with the men, but is sent back to the women and children.

6. The next morning, the men are made to carry supplies for the soldiers.

7. After the women and children leave the rebel camp, they find shelter for the night in a barn.

8. When Salva wakes up, he finds that everyone has left him behind. He is alone.

Chapter 2 Extension/Discussion Question Answers:

Sample answer: The people may have left Salva behind because he was not part of their families and they thought that an extra child might be too much of a burden to take care of. This had to be a hard choice for them to make. If I had children, I would want to take care of them as best I could, and that might mean not helping others when it could hurt my own family. But if I were Salva, I would feel horrible about being deserted like that.

Chapter 3 Comprehension Question Answers:

1. The pond where Nya gets water is busy and muddy. There are lots of other women and girls there getting water and also lots of animals such as birds and cattle there drinking from the pond.

2. The water does not sound good to drink. It says the water is muddy and brown, which does not sound healthy.

3. Nya puts a cloth doughnut on her head, puts the jug of water on top of that and uses one hand to balance the jug as she carries it on her head.

4. Salva thinks the others left him behind because he is a child and might tire too quickly and slow down the group, or complain and cause other problems.

5. When Salva leaves the barn, he sees smoke from bombs far away. Then he sees a small pond, a house, and a woman sitting outside.

6. Salva can tell the woman is part of his tribe from the pattern of scars on her face.

7. The woman gives Salva two handfuls of raw peanuts when he first approaches.

8. Salva stays with the woman for four days.

9. The woman tells Salva that she must go to a different village near water, and that it will be safer for her to travel alone.

10. As Salva is sitting in the barn pondering the woman's words, he hears a small group of people walking toward the house. He is excited to realize that these people are also from his tribe.

Chapter 3 Extension/Discussion Question Answers:

Sample Answer: Since the area is at war, the woman may not be happy to see any stranger, since they could bring trouble. Also, it seems that there is not a lot to share and the woman may not want to share what she has with Salva.

Chapter 4 Comprehension Question Answers:

1. Nya's mother puts the water into three large jars.

2. Nya eats a bowl of boiled sorghum meal with a little milk on it.

3. Nya's mother tells her to take her little sister, Akeer, with her when she walks back to the pond.

4. The strangers say that Salva will slow them down and they already have a difficult time finding food. They also say that he is too young to do any real work.

5. The man agrees because a woman (maybe his wife) seemed to want to do so and he says that Salva is Dinka. He is a member of their tribe, so they will care for him.

6. The old woman gives Salva a bag of peanuts and a gourd to use for drinking water.

7. A group of people from another tribe, called the Jur-chol, join the group after about a week of walking.

8. The young man Salva walks next to is a Jur-chol whose name is Buksa.

9. Buksa finds a bee hive full of honey for the group.

Chapter 4 Extension/Discussion Question Answers:

1. Nya does not want to take her sister to the pond because she is small and walks too slow. This is much like one of the reasons that the strangers do not want to take Salva with them.

Chapter 5 Comprehension Question Answers:

1. The big lake is three days' walk from Nya's village.

2. Nya's family doesn't live by the big lake all the time because there is fighting there between her tribe and the Dinka tribe over the land around the lake.

3. To fetch water at the lake, Nya has to dig a deep hole and wait for it to fill with water. Then she scoops out the water and waits for more.

4. When the group went to get the beehive, they were attacked by the bees and many of the men, including Salva, were stung.

5. One man cannot enjoy the honey because he was stung on the tongue and cannot swallow.

6. Salva meets Marial when Salva accidentally steps on Marial's hand one evening and the two realize that they are both alone within the group.

7. The group is headed to Ethiopia.

8. The Dinka call the Atuot "the people of the lion" because they live in an area where there are lions and the Dinka believe that when an Atuot person dies, he comes back as a lion that hungers for human flesh.

Chapter 5 Extension/Discussion Question Answers:

Answers will vary. Sample answer: Now that Salva has a friend in the group, he will probably be less discouraged because he has someone to talk to and laugh with. This will help him stay motivated to keep moving even when facing obstacles. It also shows him that there are others like him.

Chapter 6 Comprehension Question Answers:

1. Nya likes the lake camp because she does not have to walk far for water.

2. When the family is at the lake camp, Nya's mother is afraid that the men in their family will meet up with men from the Dinka tribe and fight them, getting hurt or killed.

3. Salva's Uncle Jewiir calls his name.

4. Uncle Jewiir had been with the group for three days before finding Salva.

5. Uncle Jewiir has a gun, so he is able to hunt for the group.

6. Salva is up sick most of one night because he ate too much and ate it too fast. Because he had not had much food in a while, eating so much food quickly hurt his stomach.

7. Uncle Jewiir wakes Salva up and tells him that his friend (Marial) is gone.

Chapter 6 Extension/Discussion Question Answers:

1. Since someone else is crying when Uncle wakes Salva, whatever happened to Marial must have also happened to someone else. Marial had no family travelling with him, so no one would be crying over him except for his friend, Salva.

Chapter 7 Comprehension Question Answers:

1. Nya is worried about Akeer because she is very sick and although many who get this illness recover enough to work, it often kills small children.

2. Nya's family must decide if they are going to take Akeer to the nearest medical clinic, which is many miles away or if they are going to let her rest in camp and hope she heals on her own.

3. Salva thinks Marial was taken by a hungry lion.

4. To get to Ethiopia, the group must cross the Nile River.

5. The group works together to make boats out of reed to cross the Nile.

6. Salva helps with the boat building by gathering cut reeds and carrying them to the boat builders.

Chapter 8 Comprehension Question Answerss:

1. Nya's family decides to take Akeer to the medical clinic.

2. The family is told to boil their water for a count of two hundred to make is safe to drink.

3. This will be difficult while they are at the lake camp because they are only able to get a little water at a time and it will have boiled away before a count of two hundred.

4. The group stops on an island where some fishermen live.

5. Uncle shares some sugar cane and fish and yams with Salva.

6. Salva remembers his father bringing mangoes from the marketplace as a treat. Since his bicycle was always filled with other things they needed, he would put the mangoes in the spokes of his bicycle wheels.

7. Just after the fishermen go into their tents, mosquitoes cover the island biting anyone who is not safe within mosquito netting.

8. The travelers are warned to take a lot of water on the next part of their journey, since they will be crossing a desert.

Chapter 8 Extension/Discussion Question Answers:

Answers will vary.

Chapter 9 Comprehension Question Answers:

1. Two men show up in a jeep and talk to the village chief about water.

2. Uncle says it will take three days to cross the desert.

3. At the end of the first day in the desert, Salva stubs his toe and his whole toenail comes off.

4. Uncle keeps Salva going by choosing near-by landmarks and asking him to walk to those, so that the journey doesn't seem so far.

5. On their second day of crossing the desert, the group comes across a group of men who have collapsed on the sand and have no water.

Chapter 9 Extension/Discussion Question Answers:

Answers will vary.

Chapter 10 Comprehension Question Answers:

1. The two men say that water will be found between the two trees in the village.

2. The men that are given water are able to get up and join the group as they continue walking.

3. Salva asks his uncle how his family will find him if he is in Ethiopia. Uncle replies his family probably did not survive the attack on the village.

4. Uncle tells Salva that once they reach the refugee camp, he is going back to Sudan to fight.

5. Uncle gives Salva hope that he will see his family again by telling him he will talk to people as he travels and ask about Salva's family.

6. The group finds a dead stork by a small muddy puddle, and they decide to cook it.

7. A group of six men of the Nuer tribe with guns and machetes comes up and robs the people and kills Uncle.

Chapter 10 Extension/Discussion Question Answers:

1. Answers may vary. Sample answer:

    I believe that Salva would have shared his water. During his journey, he has been helped by others and he has been very grateful for that and has also wanted to prove that he can be a man. He could prove himself by sharing what he has with another while also repaying the debt he owes to others who have helped him along the way.

2. Answers may vary.

Chapter 11 Comprehension Question Answers:

1. The villagers start clearing more of the land between the two trees after the two men in the jeep leave.

2. The group buries Uncle in a hole about two feet deep that had been dug by an animal.

3. The stork the group was cooking was eaten by other birds while the group was being robbed.

4. Now that Uncle and Marial are both gone, Salve becomes more determined to survive because he feels that is what they both would have wanted. He feels as if the two of them have left him their strength.

5. Once Uncle is dead, the group stops sharing food with Salva unless he begs for it and no one really talks to him.

6. When Salva reaches the refugee camp, he sees more people than he has ever seen gathered in one place before.

7. On his second day in camp, Salva thinks he sees his mother and he goes to catch up with her.

Chapter 12 Comprehension Question Answers:

1. The red iron giraffe is a drill.

2. The rocks are broken up into gravel.

3. As Salva is trying to catch up to the woman in the orange headscarf, he realizes that his family is likely dead.

4. Salva lives at the refugee camp for six years.

5. Salva is seventeen when the camp is closed.

6. The people of the camp are chased to the Gilo River by the soldiers.

7. The dangers of the Gilo River are the strong current from the rainy season and the crocodiles.

Chapter 13 Comprehension Question Answers:

1. Nya thinks it is funny that you have to use water to find water.

2. The drilling crew is discouraged when the plastic bag used to hold water keeps getting leaks in it.

3. The boss, who is one of the two men who came in the jeep, keeps the workers going.

4. The young man that Salva watches jump into the river is eaten by a crocodile.

5. Salva is finally forced into the water by the shooting soldiers.

6. Another boy grabs onto Salva as he is swimming across the river, pushing him under the water. While the boy is holding Salva under, he is shot by one of the soldiers, which saves Salva's life.

7. Salva decides to walk to the south toward Kenya.

8. As Salva is walking, other boys start to follow him and he becomes the leader of the group.

9. Salva decides the group needs to travel at night and hide during the day to stay safer from the bombing and fighting.

10. Twelve hundred boys make it safely to Kenya. It takes a year and a half to get there.

Chapter 13 Extension/Discussion Question Answers:

1. Salva's memories of his family help him to keep the boys organized and moving. He remembers how he took care of his little brother, and treats the younger boys in a similar fashion. He remembers how his older brothers would talk in a way that made him feel he must listen, and how his sisters were gentle with him. He remembers his father's strength and how his mother cared for him. And he remembers how his uncle kept him going by asking him to just take it one step at a time.

Chapter 14 Comprehension Question Answers:

1. On the third afternoon of drilling in the village, the drill finds water which shoots in the air.

2. Nya frowns because the water that is coming out of the ground is brown and muddy, not water they can drink.

3. Salva is twenty-two years old in this chapter.

4. Kakuma is in the middle of a dry desert and is surrounded by barbed wire. No one is allowed to go outside the fence unless they are leaving the camp and not returning. The local people do not like having the camp nearby and come to steal from the refugees in the camp.

5. Salva stays at Kakuma for two years.

6. After he leaves Kakuma, Salva goes to a camp at Ifo.

7. Michael, a man from Ireland, teaches Salva to read and play volleyball.

8. A rumor spread through the camp that some boys and younger men from the camps would be going to live in America.

9. According to the aid workers, those who are chosen to go to America must be healthy orphans who have never been soldiers.

10. According to the list, Salva is going to Rochester, New York.

Chapter 14 Extension/Discussion Question Answers:

1. Sample Answer: Like Salva, I knew how to speak English before I learned how to read and write. I learned my letters first, just like Salva did, too, but I learned the letters one at a time. Salva learns A,B, & C together. Salva had already learned to read and write in another language (Arabic) before learning English, but I learned English first. I was able to practice my letters on paper, but Salva practices with a stick in the dirt.

Chapter 15 Comprehension Question Answers:

1. Dep says the water coming from the borehole is muddy because it is mixed with the water that was used for drilling.

2. The orphans like Salva are being called "Lost Boys."

3. From Ifo, Salva goes to Nairobi, the capital of Kenya to prepare for his journey to America.

4. The one thing Salva remembers clearly is being given new clothes. He is given so many clothes that he is surprised to hear he is supposed to wear them all at the same time.

5. Salva drinks Coca-Cola on the plane, and it reminds him of the time his father brought home a few bottles of it for his family.

6. Salva has to take three planes to get to his new home.

7. Salva's new family consists of Chris, the dad; Louise, the mom; and four other children.

Chapter 15 Extension/Discussion Question Answers:

1. Answers may vary. Sample answer:

Salva stops just inside the doors of the airport before leaving because he realizes he is leaving his old life behind him. Once he walks through the doors of the airport, he will be joining his new family in a new life in a new country. Before this moment, he hadn't been close enough to his goal to really feel that he was truly starting fresh.

Chapter 16 Comprehension Question Answers:

1. The men of the village start clearing another area past one of the big trees.

2. Salva has not seen any dirt roads in the month he has been in Rochester.

3. Salva focuses on his lessons to block out the confusion of his new life.

4. It had taken Salva four days to get from Ifo to Rochester.

5. Salva decides to study business in college.

6. The e-mail from his cousin tells Salva that his father in alive and in a clinic where he is recovering from stomach surgery.

7. It takes months to get Salva's trip back to Sudan organized.

Chapter 16 Extension/Discussion Question Answers:

1. Answers will vary. Possible examples of frustrating English inconsistencies:
   Plural of mouse = mice, but plural of house = houses
   Plural of foot = feet, but plural of book = books
   Words that are spelled different but pronounced the same (homophones)

2. Sample answer: For Salva, his time in Sudan is still very real for him and he remembers it very well, but at the same time, his new life seems a little more real and fresh for him. Perhaps it's like his new life has pushed aside his old one.

Chapter 17 Comprehension Question Answers:

1. Nya's father tells her a school is being built.

2. It has been almost nineteen years since Salva and his father had seen each other.

3. Salva's mother and sisters are back in the village. Only one of his brothers, Ring, is still alive.

4. Salva's father is sick from years of drinking dirty water that was infested with guinea worms.

5. The first time Salva speaks in front of an audience to raise money for his project, he thinks about the meetings he would have with the boys that followed him to Kenya and realizes that these people, just like the boys, are interested in what he has to say.

Chapter 17 Extension/Discussion Question Answers:

1. When Nya's father tells her all the children, even the girls, will be able to attend the new school, it shows a change in Sudan from when Salva was a boy. Salva's sisters and the other girls of his village stayed home with their mothers to learn how to keep house. None of them went to school like Nya will be able to. Perhaps the people of Sudan have realized the value of educating as many of their people as possible.

Chapter 18 Comprehension Question Answers:

1. The leader of the workers brings out a big sign for the people to hold up for pictures before the well is used for the first time. It is to honor the school in America that raised the money for the well.

2. Nya's uncle is working the well when she gets water from it for the first time. He gets this honor because he is the chief of the village.

3. Because of the new well, the new school is being built. There is also talk that there will be a market built the next year with a medical clinic possibly in the future. People from all around the area will come to the village to get clean water from the well.

4. Dep surprises Nya by telling her that the leader of the work crew is a Dinka.

5. Nya thanks the leader of the work crew.

6. Salva is the leader of the work crew.

A Message from Salva Dut Comprehension Questions:

1. Salva thanks the United Nations and the International Red Cross for helping him when he was in danger of starving.

2. Salva went to college at Monroe Community College.

3. Salva's project is Water for Sudan, Inc.

4. Salva says that hope and perseverance helped him to overcome his difficulties.

A Message From Salva Dut Extension/Discission Questions:

1. Answers will vary. This discussion question can easily be turned into a compare/contrast essay prompt.

Comprehension Test—*A Long Walk To Water*

1. This novel is set mainly in:
   A. Egypt   B. Sudan   C. The United States   D. the Nile

2. The main male character in this novel is named:
   A. Dep   B. Akobo   C. Salva   D. Jewiir

3. The main female character in this novel is named:
   A. Nya   B. Akit   C. Akeer   D. Salva

4. Nya's job each day is to:
   A. care for her sister   B. get water   C. tend the cattle   D. cook and clean

5. Salva has to leave his home because of:
   A. disease   B. hunger   C. dirty water   D. war

6. How many times each day does Nya have to walk to the pond?
   A. one   B. two   C. three   D. as many as possible

7. Salva is a member of this tribe:
   A. Nuer   B. Jur-chol   C. Dinka   D. Atuot

8. Nya is a member of this tribe:
   A. Nuer   B. Jur-chol   C. Dinka   D. Atuot

9. This friend of Salva's disappears during their journey to Ethiopia.
   A. Nya   B. Buska   C. Atuot   D. Marial

10. During the dry season, Nya's family moves to:
    A. the Nile   B. the lake   C. Ethiopia   D. America

11. The only family member that Salva finds on his journey to Ethiopia is:
    A. his younger brother   B. his cousin   C. his uncle   D. no one

12. Nya's sister and Salva's father are both made sick by this:
    A. dirty water   B. lack of food   C. injuries   D. the heat

13. Salva is left alone again on his journey to Ethiopia when:
    A. he gets lost   B. he runs away   C. uncle is shot   D. he is taken by soldiers

14. Life in Nya's village changes when some men come and:
    A. bring food   B. drill a well   C. build a school   D. give them money

15. When the camp in Ethiopia is closed, Salva leads a group of boys to:
    A. Uganda   B. Egypt   C. Northern Sudan   D. Kenya

16. This person teaches Salva to read English:
    A. Nya   B. Michael   C. Buska   D. Marial

17. What does Salva have to drink on the airplane to America?
    A. orange juice   B. water   C. Coca Cola   D. nothing

18. What did Salva's father bring back from the market in the spokes of his bicycle tires?
    A. pears   B. peaches   C. mangoes   D. coconuts

19. What city in America does Salva move to?

    A. New York   B. Rochester   C. Lexington   D. Frankfurt

20. What does Nya's village plan to build when the well is completed?

    A. a school   B. new homes   C. irrigation ditches   D. another well

21. Who does Salva go to visit in a clinic in Sudan?

    A. Nya   B. his father   C. uncle   D. Buska

22. What does Nya find funny about the process of digging a well?

    A. it is noisy   B. it takes too long   C. it requires water   D. it smells bad

23. Who is the man who leads the well drilling crew?

    A. Salva   B. Salva's father   C. Nya's uncle   D. Dep

24. Why does Nya feel she must thank the Dinka man?

    A. because he is from a different tribe that does not get along with her tribe

    B. because he has been so nice to her

    C. because she is afraid no one else will thank him

    D. because she heard he has had a hard life

25. What does Salva say helped him to overcome the difficulties in his life?

    A. hope and faith   B. persistence and strength

    C. love and family   D. hope and perseverance

Comprehension Test Answer Key—*A Long Walk To Water*

1. B

2. C

3. A

4. B

5. D

6. B

7. C

8. A

9. D

10. B

11. C

12. A

13. C

14. B

15. D

16. B

17. C

18. C

19. B

20. A

21. B

22. C

23. A

24. A

25. D

Further Reading about The Lost Boys of Sudan:

Ajak, Benjamin; Deng, Benson; Deng, Alphonsian; & Bernstein, Judy. *They Poured Fire on Us From The Sky.* Public Affairs, 2006.

Bixler, Mark. *The Lost Boys of Sudan: An American Story of the Refugee Experience.* University of Georgia Press, 2006.

Burlingame, Jeff. *The Lost Boys of Sudan (Great Escapes).* Benchmark Books, 2011.

Dau, John Bul. *Lost Boy, Lost Girl: Escaping Civil War in Sudan.* National Geographic Children's Books, 2010.

Disco, James; Clark, Susan; & Singleton, Niki. *Echoes of the Lost Boys of Sudan.* Brown Books Publishing Group, 2011.

Eggers, Dave. *What is the What?* Vintage, 2007.

Hecht, Joan. *The Journey of the Lost Boys: A Story of Courage, Faith, and the Sheer Determination to Survive by a Group of Young Boys Called "The Lost Boys of Sudan."* Allswell Press, 2005.

Lomong, Lopez & Tabb. Mark. *Running For My Life: One Lost Boy's Journey From the Killing Fields of Sudan to the Olympic Games.* Thomas Nelson, 2012.

Makeer, Joseph Akol. *From Africa to America: The Journey of a Lost Boy of Sudan.* Tate Publishing & Enterprises, 2008.

Nhial, Abraham. *Lost Boy No More: A True Story of Survival and Salvation.* B&H Books, 2004.

Vincent, David Nyuol & Nader, Carol. *The Boy Who Wouldn't Die.* Allen & Unwin, 2012.

Williams, Mary. *Brothers in Hope: The Story of the Lost Boys of Sudan.* Lee & Low Books, 2005.

Youree, Barbara; Leek, Ayuel; & Ngor, Beny. *Courageous Journey: Walking the Lost Boys' Path From Sudan to America.* New Horizon Press, 2008.

If you liked this novel unit, check out these other titles all available on Amazon!

Novel Unit for *The Mostly True Adventures of Homer P. Figg*

ISBN-13: 978-1478204985

This novel unit contains everything you need to teach the novel *The Mostly True Adventures of Homer P. Figg* by Rodman Philbrick.
Includes vocabulary, comprehension and discussion questions for each chapter, vocabulary practice exercises, pre, during, and post reading activities, and essay topics. Also contains tests, additional activity and research activities, a list of suggested further reading (both fiction & nonfiction), and a listing of the 6-12 Common Core Anchor Standards of Language Arts covered in the novel.

Novel Unit for *The Graveyard Book* by Neil Gaiman

ISBN-13: 978-1477695753

The Graveyard Book by Neil Gaiman is an exciting and suspenseful book about Nobody Owens, a boy orphaned when his family is murdered. To keep him safe from the man who killed his family, Nobody is taken in by the residents of the local graveyard, and there his adventures begin. This novel unit includes vocabulary, comprehension questions & higher level discussion questions for each chapter (with answer keys), a bank of test questions, additional research, writing, and language activities, essay topics, and during and after reading project activity suggestions. Includes vocabulary word search, review crossword, and rhyming riddle puzzles that will challenge your students! Also includes a page listing the Common Core Standards covered by the activities included in the novel guide.

Novel Unit for *Aliens on Vacation* by Clete Barrett Smith

ISBN-13: 978-1478299783

This novel unit contains everything you need to teach the novel Aliens on Vacation by Clete Barrett Smith. Includes vocabulary, comprehension and discussion questions for each chapter, vocabulary practice exercises, pre, during, and post reading activities, and essay topics. Also contains tests, additional research activities and other activities in language arts, science, and math, and a listing of the K-5 Common Core Anchor Standards of Language Arts covered in the novel.

Dread Locks: A Novel Guide

ISBN-13: 978-1475277920

Dread Locks by Neal Shusterman is a great novel for middle grades students. The story mixes mythology and fairy tales to create an edge-of-your-seat novel that students will love to read and discuss. The novel also gives opportunities for lessons on foreshadowing, figurative language, and making predictions.
With this teacher created novel unit, you'll be ready to jump right in with vocabulary, comprehension and discussion questions, extension activities, and a bank of test questions based on the novel.

Haiku Is For Wimps: A Poetry Unit

ISBN-13: 978-1475227291

Tired of teaching the same boring forms of poetry to your students? Want poetic forms that will challenge them, but are still fun? Look no further! This poetry unit will help you teach your students to write a terza rima, sestina, & villanelle. It is a complete unit with examples, student worksheets, and suggested topics for each type of poem. The lessons in this teacher guide give students an opportunity to go beyond the usual and to meet the challenges of more rigorous poetic forms.

Made in the USA
Lexington, KY
25 May 2013